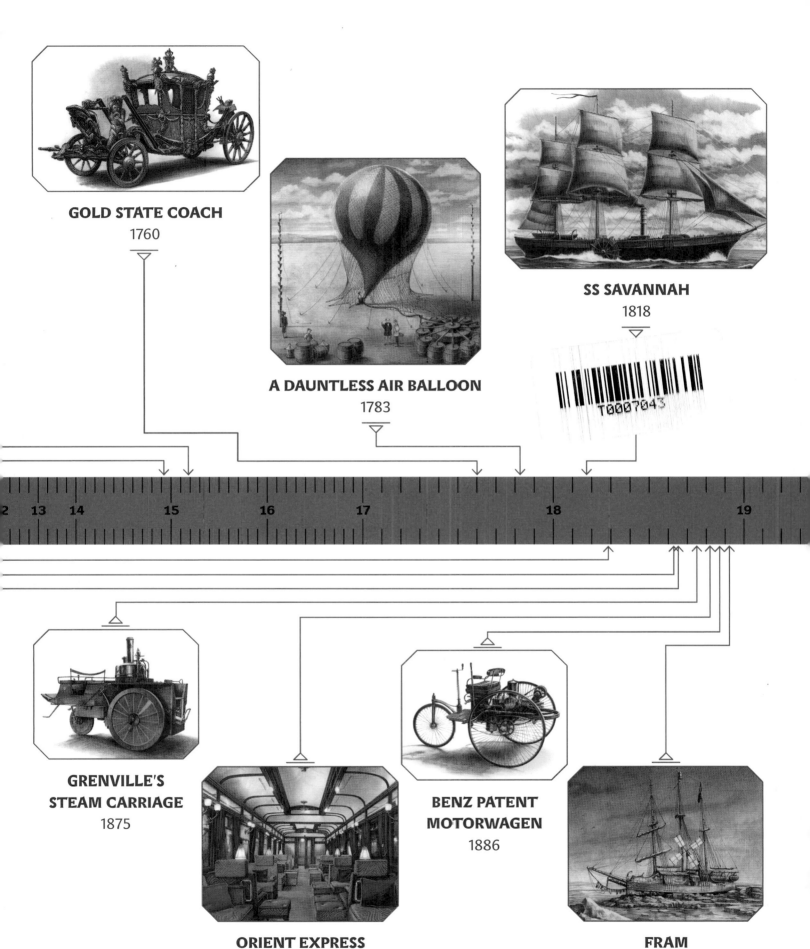

GOLD STATE COACH
1760

A DAUNTLESS AIR BALLOON
1783

SS SAVANNAH
1818

T0007043

2 13 14 15 16 17 18 19

GRENVILLE'S STEAM CARRIAGE
1875

ORIENT EXPRESS
1883

BENZ PATENT MOTORWAGEN
1886

FRAM
1892

MEANS OF
TRANSPORT THAT
CHANGED THE WORLD

Albatros

The Battle of Fleurus – page 16

TABLE OF CONTENTS

INTRODUCTION

We all travel sometimes—to school, to see a friend in another town, perhaps even to a foreign country on vacation. Have you ever wondered how people traveled centuries ago, and what earlier generations had to do to get from place to place? Today we take cars for granted, but in earlier times a car was a fantasy, at best an idea. But all grand schemes begin with an idea. Once upon a time someone had the idea of crossing the open sea in search of new routes to faraway lands, using nothing but the wind, paddles, and a few tons of wood. Today, the ships that battled the ocean waves are in museums or at the bottom of the sea. The modern vessels of today are at peace with the sea: they are far larger than their predecessors and can move without the wind's help, something the first seafarers would have found fantastical. What if our ancestors had learned that birds are not the only creatures that can fly, because we terrestrial bipeds can transport thousands of people from one end of the planet to another? And that we can even fly beyond our own world, into outer space? Maybe one of our young readers will be inspired by these pages enough to come up with an idea so grand that people of the future will write about it. Who knows?

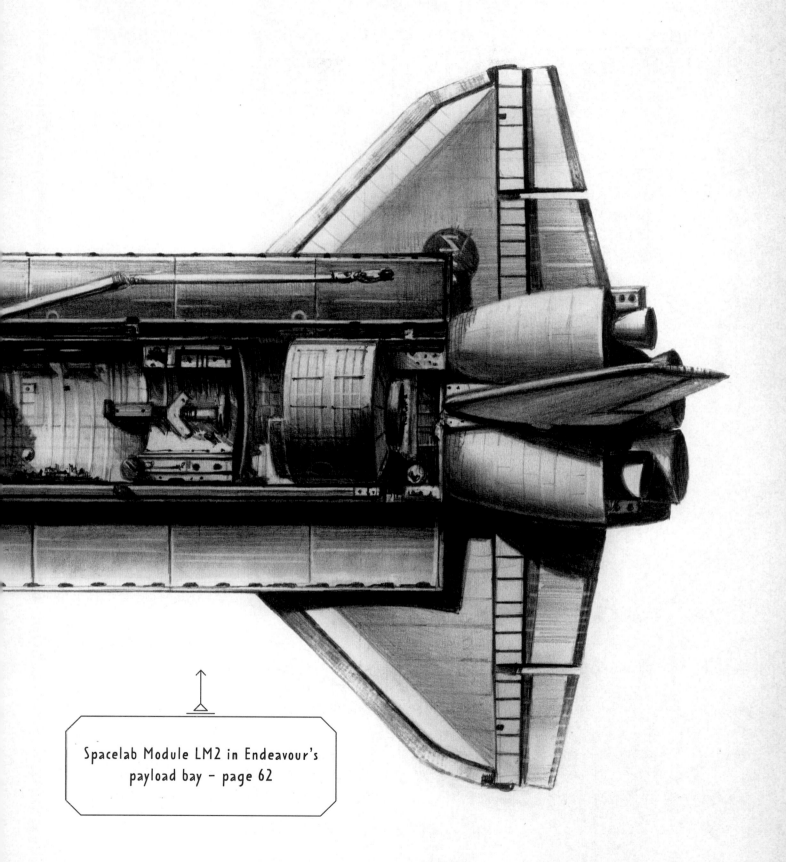

Spacelab Module LM2 in Endeavour's
payload bay – page 62

TESSARA-KONTERES

The galley *Tessarakonteres* is undoubtedly the largest non-motorized ship the world has ever seen. Although commissioned by the pharaoh Ptolemy IV, who ruled Egypt from 221 to 204 BCE, this enormous ship—over 400 feet long—was not built in Egypt. At Ptolemy's request, it was constructed and named in Ancient Greece. The name is loosely translated as forty or forty-rowed, for the forty rowers on each column of oars that propelled this huge ship. "Forty rowers?" you say. "That's not so many." How wrong you are! The oars they used were no ordinary light or mid-weight paddles; they were great logs of wood, each of which needed eight strong men to work it! As there were 80 oars in total—40 on each side—the ship had to be powered by 640 oarsmen, most of whom were prisoners. For

Oars in three banks (trireme) - from the top: thranites, zygites, thalamites

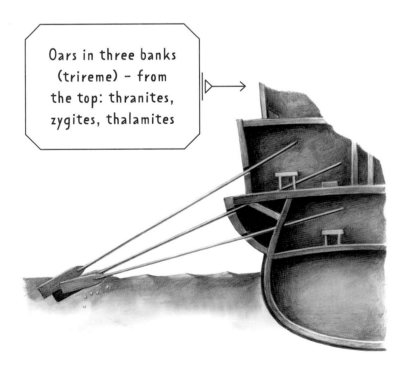

The ship may have looked like this. Due to a lack of historical evidence, we can only speculate about its appearance.

a single voyage, 640 oarsmen were too few, however. So that they could eat, sleep, rest, and recover their strength, they had to take turns rowing. Multiply 640 by six and you get to 4,000—and that was the number of oarsmen on board. Then add to this 400 crew and a further 2,850—the number of soldiers *Tessarakonteres* could transport. Indeed, it was built to take soldiers from place to place. As you can see, then, this rowing boat was pretty massive. How fine it would have been to seen it, and to walk across its deck! It would have surely seemed like you were in a floating city. What a pity we will never have the opportunity! *Tessarakonteres*, this showcase of Ptolemy's power, is with us no longer. Indeed, we can't be sure that she ever truly existed.

NEMI SHIPS

The Roman emperor Caligula is perhaps the most notorious figure of Ancient Rome. He is the emperor who had his horse appointed a senator, who carried on long debates with the moon, and who had a preference for occult rituals. So great was his admiration for Diana (goddess of the hunt, the moon, and chastity) that he decided to build two enormous ships at Lake Nemi and dedicate them to her. At certain times, the lake reflects the moon to breathtaking effect, which explains why it was known as Diana's Mirror. The problem was, as no river flowed into the lake, it was impossible to reach by boat. We still don't know how Caligula's ships were carried to the lake. What we do know—from wrecks that ended up on the lakebed, forgotten like the rule of the mad emperor—is that the ships were magnificent floating palaces, surely wonders of the world. They were plentifully adorned with statues

It was basically a floating palace with marble decor, works of art, mosaic flooring, plumbing, heating, gardens, and bathrooms. Many of the ship's conveniences seemed to come from a later age.

made from precious metals, and they contained drainage and water systems and spas. Fishermen continued to pull treasures from the lake for centuries; even today, archaeologists dream of retrieving fragments of mad Caligula's incredible ships. In 1446, a young cardinal and nephew of the Pope named Prospero Colonna attempted to pull one of the ships ashore with ropes, but he succeeded in retrieving only a few rotten beams. In 1535, Italian inventors Guglielmo de Lorena and Francesco de Marchi had more luck when they boldly set out to explore the ships underwater in an invention known as a diving bell. By their actions, these two daredevils unwittingly laid the foundations of modern diving. It wasn't until the years of World War II, however, that the colossal ships (over 240 feet long) were at last pulled from the lake, after Italian dictator Benito Mussolini had the lake drained. The ships were taken to Rome, where they came to a sorry end in the final days of the war, when the Italian capital was bombarded. Pride comes before a fall, they say—as two despotic Italian rulers can surely attest.

Lake Nemi, which is in the Alban Hills about 20 miles south of Rome, is of volcanic origin.

The astronomer Edmond Halley, for whom Halley's Comet is named, invented a diving bell that used barrels filled with oxygen.

SANTA MARÍA

The prow of the *Santa María* ploughed into the sand of a New World. Having jumped overboard along with his crew, the leader of the expedition, the celebrated Christopher Columbus, was about to speak. "Gentleman," he declared, "we have reached the shores of the Indies, of this I am sure. I am also sure that we are the first men ever to have reached this continent." These may not have been Columbus's exact words, but the sentiment is about right. Truth be told, however, the *Niña*, the *Pinta*, and the *Santa María* had discovered the shores not of Asia but of an island off the coast of the Americas. This explains why Columbus referred, wrongly, to the local population as Indians. America became America less than thirty years later, named for Italian navigator Amerigo Vespucci. Columbus's second assertion isn't altogether correct either. A full five centuries earlier, a party of Vikings led by Leif Eriksson had set foot on the shores of North America. The Vikings were well known for their sturdy Drakkar longships, which were extremely advanced for their time. They used the wind as their main source of propulsion, supplementing it with the work of oarsmen. The

From left: the PINTA, the SANTA MARÍA and the NIÑA

A Drakar longship

unique hull of the Drakkar was made from wet wood bent over fire. Thus equipped, the dreaded Norsemen succeeded in conquering the land. Remarkably, the far newer *Santa María* wasn't much more powerful than the centuries-old Drakkar. If you are thinking of it as a ship of great magnificence, you are as much mistaken as Columbus was with his misidentification of the Indies.

The *Santa María* was the slowest ship in the expedition and was not particularly large. Although only its anchor survives today, historians believe that it was only about 85 feet long. Some moments in history simply aren't as they first appear. What we can say for sure about Columbus, however, is that his expedition changed our world once and for all.

VICTORIA

MAGELLAN'S CIRCUMNAVIGATION

1. Sanlúcar de Barrameda, Spain – September 20, 1519
2. Santa Lucia Bay – December 13, 1519
3. Río de Solis – January 12, 1520
4. Strait of Magellan – October 21, 1520
5. Kingdom of Mactan, Philippines – April 27, 1521. Ferdinand Magellan died
6. Ambon Island – December 21, 1521. Juan Sebastián Elcano became captain

Believe it or not, people used to believe that our planet was as flat as a pancake, and that if you were to reach the end of it, you would fall into space. This assumption was at last refuted in the early 16th century, when an expedition led by Portuguese navigator Fernão de Magalhães (known to us as Ferdinand Magellan) achieved the first circumnavigation of the Earth. But Magellan never made it home: he died in battle in the Philippines, having become embroiled in a fight with native tribes, whom he had been trying to forcibly convert to Christianity. Only one of the five ships that set out on the expedition from Spanish harbors in 1519 returned. It was left to the *Victoria* to bring this groundbreaking three-year expedition to a successful conclusion. As a large merchant ship called a *carrack*, it first crossed the Atlantic Ocean to the southern tip of the South American continent—a tip that has since become known as the Strait of Magellan. After that, it sailed the Pacific to the Philippines. Not only the leader of the expedition met his end there; so, too, did the ship the *Concepción*. Chaos, skirmishes, and constant changes in command resulted in the order to burn the ship and abandon the expedition. The *Victoria* was left as the sole surviving vessel. With only fifty sailors on board, it sailed around Australia and Africa on its return to European waters. The *Victoria* would make two more trips to North America. On the second of these, it would perish. The first ship to circumnavigate the Earth now rests in peace somewhere at the bottom of the Atlantic.

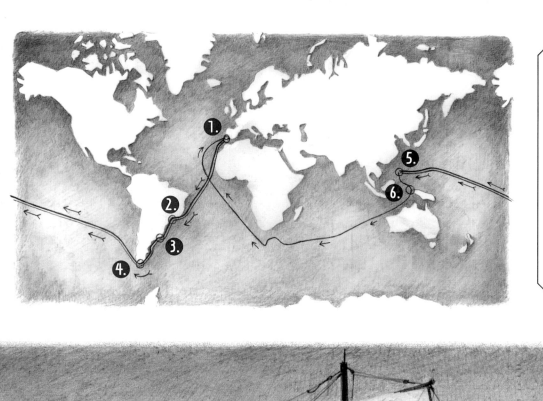

Of the five ships that set off on the voyage, only the VICTORIA completed the circumnavigation. TRINIDAD: captured in the Moluccas; SAN ANTONIO: deserted in South America; CONCEPCION: burned by natives in the Philippines; SANTIAGO: wrecked off South America.

GOLD STATE COACH

As the Gold State Coach weighs four tons, it must be pulled by eight horses. It is on view to the public at the Royal Mews at Buckingham Palace.

Had you attended every coronation of a British monarch, you would be almost 1,000 years old. Of course, no one can reach such a great age. Nevertheless, members of the British royal family tend to be long-lived, which means that many of us will manage only one such coronation in our lifetime. There is one thing about these coronations that hasn't changed for almost 250 years, though—and we can see it on other occasions too. It is the ceremonial coronation carriage, nicknamed the Gold State Coach. Take a look at it and you will soon see where the nickname comes from.

The Gold State Coach was designed by Samuel Butler and built in his workshops. Made to demonstrate the wealth and power of the British Empire, it is a truly impressive sight. As it was intended to last for many centuries, it is no wonder that no expense was spared in its creation. It is adorned with countless sculptures, paintings, and carvings, and it is coated in real gold. The Kingdoms of Denmark and the Netherlands today boast of similar carriages.

One thing of which the wearer of the British crown would not boast is the fact that a ride in this super-carriage is a pretty unbearable experience. King George VI declared himself to have had "one of the most uncomfortable rides I have ever had in my life" in it. Likewise, by her use of "horrible" and "not very comfortable" to describe the trip to her coronation, Queen Elizabeth II seemed to agree with him. Perhaps the carriage has remained in perfect condition for over two centuries because no one has ever volunteered to ride in it. As we travel in far greater comfort in the automobiles of today, we might expect the Gold State Coach to remain in its pristine state for some centuries to come.

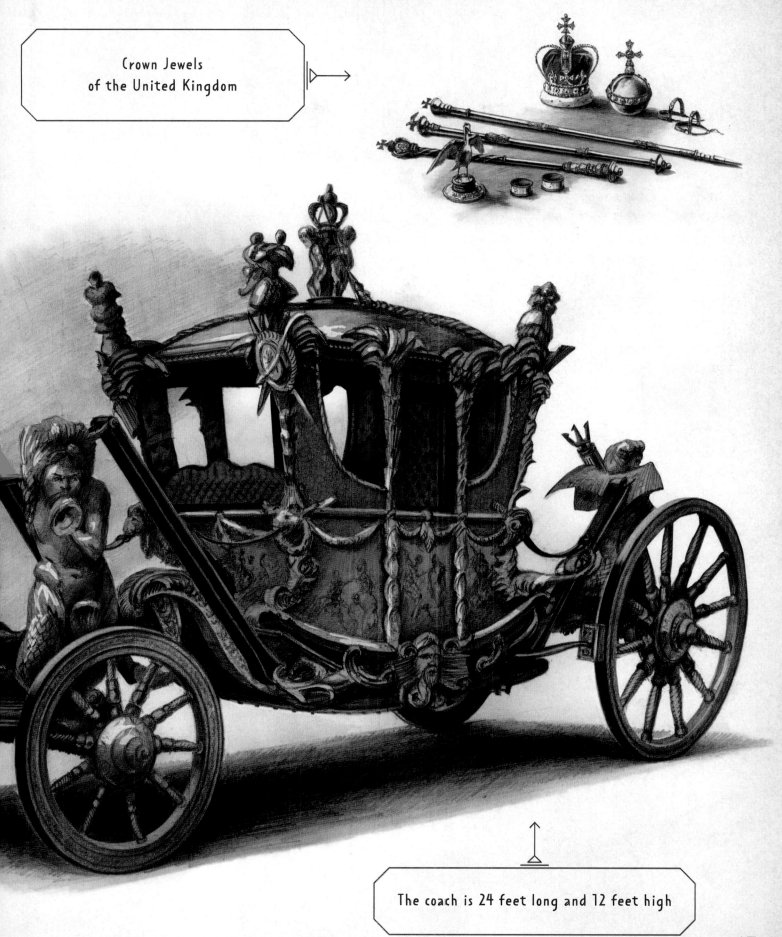

Crown Jewels
of the United Kingdom

The coach is 24 feet long and 12 feet high

A DAUNTLESS AIR BALLOON

It is a beautiful Saturday afternoon in 1783 in a small French village in the commune of Gonesse. Jean-Paul has opened a bottle of red wine, filled his pipe, and is sitting comfortably on the doorstep of his house. "What a lovely quiet summer's day!" he sighs with satisfaction. He has just lit his pipe and taken his first puff when his contemplations are disturbed by sounds reminiscent of an army on the march, followed by the sight of an angry, disorderly crowd pushing past his house. Dogs bark. Men wave pitchforks. Women scream. "By the saints, what's going on?" mutters Jean-Paul. One look at the sky is enough to tell him. As he stares up in astonishment, he doesn't realize that his pipe has fallen from his mouth. Above the fields is a large white ball, and it seems to be heading for the ground—for the land of his parents and their parents before them. "No way!" Jean-Paul growls, before grabbing his pitchfork and joining the ranks of his neighbors, advancing to combat the mysterious ball!

These simple, enraged villagers of Gonesse commune succeeded in destroying the monster with their feet and their pitchforks. But it was no monster; it was the very first hydrogen-filled balloon, and it had been in flight for 45 minutes.

Before long, gas balloons were far more common. They were filled with hydrogen transported in wooden barrels. Eleven years later, at the Battle of Fleurus, the French army monitored enemy forces using a balloon that worked on the same principle, thus helping itself to victory—making L'Intrépide the very first gas-powered vessel to determine the course of a battle.

SS SAVANNAH

The 19th century is often referred to as the Age of Steam: the technological progress of the time was accelerated by the implementation of the steam engine. Although invented in the 1st century AD by Hero of Alexandria, it was not used properly until the inventor James Watt did so in the 18th century. Thanks to Watt, a mechanism evolved that used steam in a cylinder to lift a piston, which in turn lifted other pistons, thus setting into motion a whole system of pistons, and this system became ever more widespread. It was able to move a train, even an oceangoing vessel. On her maiden voyage across the Atlantic in 1819, the SS *Savannah* became the very first steam-powered ship. Side wheels were used to

A steam engine uses steam pressure to push a piston back and forth inside a cylinder. By means of a connecting rod and a flywheel, the pushing force is converted into rotational force.

start up the ship's steam engine. For the most part, however, the *Savannah* was propelled by favorable winds in her sails. In the early days of steam power, the operation of a steam engine was a costly affair. Before long, the *Savannah* lost its side wheels and engine and came to rely solely on its sails. Even so, it was hugely influential in the development of shipping. As the 19th century wore on, the steam engine underwent many improvements that brought it into the modern world. "SS" is short for "steamship." The SS *Savannah* is the inspiration behind another feat of water transport, namely the building of the NS *Savannah* (in which the N stands for "nuclear"). In service from 1962–1972, the NS *Savannah* was the first non-warship cargo ship powered by atomic energy. It came into being thanks to the Atoms for Peace initiative. Unfortunately, it too proved very costly to operate. After a few tours in Germany and Japan, it was taken out of service. Today, the NS *Savannah* serves as a museum.

DOUBLE-DECKER BUSES

What do you think of when you hear the name London? Sherlock Holmes? Red telephone boxes? Or two-level buses? This means of transport is as much a part of England as football and fish and chips. In the 19th century, London became the world's first true metropolis. Crowds would walk the winding streets every day. So that the people could manage to get where they needed to be, in 1829 the omnibuses came into use. Pulled by horses, they carried up to 22 people on the Paddington to Bank line. Early in the 20th century, horse-drawn buses were replaced by motorized buses produced by the London General Omnibus Company, the largest player in the industry. To differentiate its buses from the competition, the LGOC painted each of its vehicles red. Later, to enable the bus to take as many passengers as possible, an upper deck was added. Thus the legendary double-decker was born. Double-deckers run to this day, operated by the same company that runs the London Underground. Each of today's London buses is equipped with satellite navigation, and some run on ecofriendly fuel. One multi-decker is associated with a strange legend. It is said that at night Londoners occasionally see a mysterious black bus, which has no scheduled point of departure or destination. Remind you of anything? You may have seen just such a bus in a film. It is the bus that saves a certain young wizard, and it has *three* decks! The bus from the film is the only drivable triple-decker bus in the world. And the young wizard's name? Harry Potter, of course! Everyone knows Harry Potter—he is as much a part of London as its red buses.

The noun OMNIBUS, referring to a long, horse-drawn vehicle, was first used by the French.

THE FIRST METRO

"**E**xcuse me, officer. Could you please direct me to the street called Moorgate?"

"Why, of course. Turn left here, then left again in five hundred yards. After that, turn right and go straight on for about twenty minutes. At the baker's at the end of the street, turn left and ask a passerby for more instructions."

The policeman's answer did nothing to alleviate the young man's confusion. How was he to find his way to the bank, where he had an appointment? "Is there no quicker way?" he asked.

"Well, you could take the omnibus," said the officer with a smile. "With two changes, you will reach your destination in about half an hour."

"But I have to be there in fifteen minutes!"

"I suppose you could try traveling underground, young man," replied the policeman, chuckling at his own joke as he made his departure.

The out-of-towner sighed: he wouldn't be getting this job, but maybe he would find another—London was the biggest city in

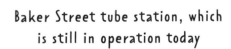

Baker Street tube station, which is still in operation today

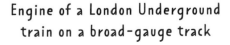

Engine of a London Underground train on a broad-gauge track

the world, after all. Many people lost their way among London's winding streets. Bearing in mind that we find ourselves at the height of the Industrial Revolution, the forerunners of today's double-deckers—omnibuses and trams—added to the overall confusion. The idea of underground travel wasn't original to the playful police officer: railway engineers were already working on the first subterranean metro. The London Underground opened on February 10, 1863, carrying 38,000 passengers—a record for the time. As trains were steam-powered, it was necessary to build an ingenious ventilation system. By the early 20th century, however, the use of electricity had developed to such a degree that the London Underground train system was as we know it today—deep in the earth, traveling at dizzying speeds.

LINCOLN'S VEHICLES

Some may think that it is great to be a head of state. All you have to do is make speeches, go to parties, and attend celebrations, while everyone listens to what you say. The truth, however, is that there is not much fun and a great deal of hard work involved. As the 16th president of the United States of America, Abraham Lincoln knew a thing or two about it. He had many troubles to contend with, not least the raging Civil War. Another of his problems was that he couldn't find a horse big enough to seat himself on. For the age in which he lived, the president was uncommonly tall. To add insult to injury, he wore an enormous top hat. When he rode onto the battlefield in support of his army, more than once he saw a soldier or two suppressing their laughter. On one occasion he was seated on such a small horse that his heels touched the ground. Such a state of affairs ill befits a president.

Now you know why Abraham Lincoln preferred to travel to important meetings by carriage. A carriage provided space in which he could stretch his long legs, relax after the demands

Abraham Lincoln's funeral train carried his coffin from Washington, DC, to Springfield, Illinois. On its three-week journey, the train stopped in seven US states.

Built in 1864 by the Wood brothers, this carriage was a gift to Abraham Lincoln before his second inauguration.

The train comprised nine coaches, including the president's, which carried Abraham Lincoln's coffin and his son's.

of the day, contemplate his next speech, and mourn the death of his eleven-year-old son. After three years of grief, he knew joy again with the end of the war. One evening in 1865, President Lincoln was at last ready for some entertainment, so he set out for Ford's Theater. As he was traveling there by carriage, little did he know that the black vehicle would enter the history books as the last he would ever ride in. At the theater, the assassin John Wilkes Booth awaited. A single shot from Booth's gun killed Mr. Lincoln. As to carriage rides, the 16th President did, in fact, take one more. The last vehicle in question was the funeral train that took the president's remains to Springfield, Illinois, where the president is buried.

GRENVILLE'S STEAM CARRIAGE

"**H**urray! We're moving along without horses to pull us! Our ancestors could only dream of a wonder such as this!" Such exclamations may have passed through the lips of the intrepid passengers of this homemade steam carriage. Designed to carry seven people, it was built in 1875 by Robert Neville Grenville, an enthusiast for all forms of motorized transport, with the assistance of his friend, the railway engineer George Jackson Churchward. The devilish machine was powered by a two-cylinder horizontal engine fueled by steam produced in a boiler into which coal was poured. The proud driver steered the vehicle by a special shaft attached to one of the front wheels and the throttle control rod. If he wished, he could engage a reverse gear and drive this colossus backwards. If he felt that he had accelerated too sharply, he could step on the brake and whistle out a warning to give other road users time to get out of the way.

Not all passengers on Grenville's steam carriage could relax and enjoy the passing landscape. A volunteer was needed to assist the driver by keeping the steam engine well watered, thus maintaining the vehicle's speed. In full flow, Grenville's machine built up such a head of steam that it was difficult to see through the smoke. I'm sure you will agree that this was less than convenient, but even so, for its time the steam carriage was a real marvel. After all, it was the first means of public transport that needed no animal to power it. Grenville's carriage conveyed delighted passengers along the roads of England, around Glastonbury, for a good twenty years. After that, it served for some time as a source of power at a local cider works.

27

ORIENT EXPRESS

The guard blew his whistle. The wheels of the train began to move. Steam rose from the chimney of the engine. As the platform got further and further away, the passengers gradually gave up waving to their loved ones before settling down in their lavish compartments. This was more or less the scene on June 5, 1883, when the first luxury train on the *Orient Express* line left the Gare de l'Est in Paris, destined for Istanbul. With its splendid compartments and lounges, it was more like a five-star hotel than a means of transport. It goes without saying that its passengers were eminent, wealthy figures.

Not even two world wars could stop it from running. With a few changes to its route, the *Orient Express* remained in operation until 2009. As time passed, carriages for ordinary mortals were added—although first-class travel on the *Orient Express* remained as magnificent as ever. This magnificence attracted thieves and other criminals, of course. The train was held up more than once, and it was even the scene of a murder. It will come as no surprise to learn that the celebrated crime writer Agatha Christie used this train as the setting for her world-famous novel, *Murder on the Orient Express.*

If you would like to find out for yourself what it was like on the Orient Express, you may. Some of its carriages have been preserved, and they make sightseeing trips. But bear in mind that the price of a single ticket is similar to the cost of a seaside holiday.

The Bar Car is one of the most impressive carriages of the *Orient Express*. With gold fittings, it was constructed in France in 1931. All passengers made a point of visiting it.

A service rather than simply a train, the Orient Express kept changing its carriages. This explains why no two are the same.

BENZ PATENT MOTORWAGEN

The life of the first vehicle powered by an internal combustion engine began in the greenhouse of its inventor, Karl Benz. This German designer worked on his car, which would change the world, at home, away from the eyes of curious onlookers. These were still the days of horse-drawn coaches, although the steam engine and the first electric cars were making such inroads that they were already recording speeds of over 60 miles per hour. How was Benz's prototype vehicle, with its maximum speed of 10 mph, to compete? Karl Benz put his automobile through its paces at night and in secret and was constantly required to iron out problems with the engine. Having made improvement upon improvement to the vehicle, at last Benz decided to apply for a patent for his invention. His application was granted.

We can say that the official date of birth of the modern automobile (i.e., a vehicle powered by an internal combustion engine) was January 29, 1886. As a fragile three-wheeler, however, Benz's car was not built for long trips. His third three-wheeler was an altogether different beast—in 1888, it managed a journey of 65 miles, which was unprecedented at the time. What's more, it was steered by Bertha Benz, making her the very first female driver. She made the drive in secret, without her husband's knowledge. Bertha had no fear of breakdowns on her long route. She cleaned out a clogged carburetor with a hairpin; she wrapped exposed wires in her garters. By this cloak-and-dagger drive along German roads—from Mannheim to Pforzheim—Bertha wished to bring her husband's pioneering vehicles to the attention of the general public. As we now know, she succeeded.

The car frame was made of steel tubes. The driver controlled the front wheel with the handle.

A single-cylinder four-stroke petrol engine with a capacity of 0.954 liters

FRAM

"**B**uild me a ship and I'll show you a current that can take it from the coastline of Siberia in the north to Greenland in the south." These words may have very well been intoned at the end of the 19th century by young Norwegian polar explorer Fridtjof Nansen. And they were enough to convince the government of Norway to have the ship built. The schooner *Fram* was three-masted, 127-feet long, and 36 feet wide. It was egg-shaped and light and there was no question of it smashing through the ice. Norway's most famous ship was launched on June 24, 1892, pushing out from the port of Oslo with a keen, intrepid crew of twelve. "We're on our way!" cried commander Nansen as they moved away from land, heading westward for the islands of Siberia. Before long, *Fram* hit ice. Nansen was not surprised, however: he had planned for this. Everything was as it should be. The ship's wide, shallow body, specially designed for the harsh polar waters, drifted through the ice with great perseverance in pursuit of its destination: the North Pole. Although the ship never reached it, it got closer than any other wooden ship had. Over the next few years, *Fram* undertook three more polar expeditions. One of them, led by the famous polar explorer Roald Amundsen, ended in success at the South Pole. We can only speculate as to how many more victories would have been chalked up on the hull of Norway's national ship had it not been for the outbreak of the First World War, which put a temporary end to all such expeditions. What we know for sure, however, is that the *Fram* sailed at each far end of the Earth.

FORD MODEL T

Henry Ford was born in 1863 in the town of Dearborn, Michigan, where he worked on a farm from a young age, like most of his neighbors. But he strongly favored taking watches apart and putting them back together over work in the fields. It was no surprise, then, that after he first saw a steam engine, on a school trip, he couldn't get the machine out of his mind. When steam engines began to appear on farms, he soon figured out how they worked. Before long, he could take them apart to the very last screw, then put them back together just as they should be.

Young Henry's technical gifts took him to the industrial city of Detroit, where he found a job as a mechanic and thus first encountered the internal combustion engine, which he came to consider as far superior to the steam engine. Henry devoted much of his time to thinking about how he could make use of this lighter, more powerful machine. Before long, he presented to local industrialists a prototype of an automobile called the Quadromobile. This vehicle had only two gears

The first mass-produced car, which was also affordable for the middle class

and four bicycle wheels. Having continued to make improvements to the Quadromobile, Ford founded his own company to manufacture cars for delighted industrialists. Unfortunately, however, a shortage of goods and reliable suppliers caused him to be fired from his own business. He was forced to start again from scratch. Rather than breaking him, however, this experience served to make Henry Ford stronger. He came up with the revolutionary idea of producing automobiles for ordinary working people, not just the rich. The production line on which parts were assembled in Ford's new factory was inspired by the practice in local slaughterhouses, whereby butchers jointed meat on a conveyor belt. He came to an arrangement with an exclusive supplier of a new type of steel. These two initiatives soon enabled him to produce a good number of automobiles quickly and cheaply. Henry Ford changed the automotive industry forever. The 20th model of his car went into production in 1920, and soon thereafter Ford became one of the world's wealthiest people. The car was known as the Model T, and practically everyone had one. How strange to recall that this story has its beginnings in Ford's taking watches apart and putting them back together again.

GRÄF & STIFT

Many means of transport have gone down in history as the first, fastest, or largest. The Double Phaeton, a sports convertible made by Austrian auto manufacturer Gräf & Stift, is remembered for very dif-

ferent reasons, however: this car was quite the mover at the outbreak of the First World War. At that crucial moment, it was an integral part of history. Weather-wise, July 28, 1914 was a glorious day. In Sarajevo, the capital of Bosnia and Herzegovina, a great military parade was in progress. How pleased the organizers must have been! Riding in the ceremonial procession were Archduke Franz Ferdinand, heir to the throne of Austria-Hungary, and his wife Sophie Chotek. Since the sun was shining, the roof of their luxury convertible was down. From their polished leather seats, the archduke and his wife were all smiles as they waved cheerily at the crowd, looking

This car had a four-cylinder engine with an output power of 28 kW.

Although the Gräf & Stift company produced different kinds of vehicles, it specialized in luxury automobiles.

Today's US presidents' cars are bulletproof and fitted with starlight cameras and tear-gas cannons.

like they hadn't a care in the world. Who could have guessed that this splendid drive would end in tragedy? Only a team of six assassins knew what was to come—they stood nervous at the roadside, awaiting their opportunity. Their plan was to blow up the car, thus sending its noble occupants to kingdom come. In this they failed: the archduke's convertible passed through the location of the planned explosion without so much as a scratch. The day might even have ended well but for some last-ditch improvisation by Gavrilo Princip, one of the six. Princip ended the lives of Franz Ferdinand and Sophie with seven well-aimed pistol shots. It is fair to say that from one moment to the next, this nineteen-year-old from Belgrade set into motion a conflict that would develop into the First World War and have everlasting consequences. And Franz Ferdinand of Austria isn't the only senior public figure to have been murdered in an automobile. On November 22, 1963, US President John F. Kennedy was dealt a fatal gunshot as he rode in a convertible in Dallas, Texas. Since this incident, heads of state no longer travel in luxury open-top vehicles. These days, they favor vehicles that look more like tanks.

TITANIC

On the night when the supposedly unsinkable *Titanic* went down, the moon and scattered stars were bright in the sky. April 14, 1912. This luxury liner was 883 feet long and 92 feet wide. It could carry 2,603 passengers, making it the largest vessel of the age. It had taken 3,000 workers an incredible three years to build and was thought to be worthy of its name, a nod to the invincible Titans of Greek mythology. It was truly enormous, weighing 48,000 tons and powered by 29 boilers and three engines controlling three propellers, allowing it to reach speeds of 26 miles per hour. The *Titanic*'s 26 watertight flood compartments and a double bottom were guarantees of its supposed invincibility. Even if four of the chambers should be punctured, it would supposedly remain comfortably afloat. It was over 100 feet high and had 10 decks. Thanks to its vast dimensions and great weight, the *Titanic* was resistant to disturbance from ocean waves; its passengers were enjoying the voyage

The TITANIC had a fully functioning plumbing system with flushing toilets. Some passengers experienced this modern convenience aboard the Titanic for the first time in their lives.

Perhaps the best-known feature of the interior was the grand staircase between the first-class decks.

without the slightest signs of seasickness. The *Titanic* wowed the public with its luxury too. Super-wealthy, first-class passengers had the use of a squash court that occupied two decks, a pool over six feet deep filled with heated sea water, a fully equipped gym, a Parisian café whose glass wall gave a view of the endless ocean, a dog-walking area, and, in the event that someone should be taken ill, a hospital with an operating theater. The sound of the engines was too low to bother anyone. Deepfreezes on the bottom deck ensured a continuous supply of the finest delicacies. For a ticket in a top-luxury cabin, passengers paid the equivalent of $128,000 dollars today. Third-class cabins were more modest, of course—instead of carved wood paneling and expensive furniture, third-class passengers made do with ordinary sturdy furniture and cheaper paneling of pine or teak. Nevertheless, third-class accommodation on the *Titanic* was considerably more opulent than third-class accommodation on other impressive ships of its time. In short, the British White Star Line's *Titanic* had set the bar very high indeed for its competitor, the Cunard Line. Or it would have, had it not vanished toward the seabed in the early morning of April 15, 1912. The *Titanic* was dogged by bad luck. Just before embarking on the voyage, a massive fire broke out in one of its coalbunkers. Then, on that fateful moonlit night, it collided with an iceberg—a collision so serious that five of the ship's flood compartments were punctured. Had the *Titanic* been equipped with searchlights, perhaps it could have prepared for the impact, and this tragedy—in which 1,500 people drowned—could have been avoided. But as searchlights were banned on merchant shipping, tragically, the unsinkable was sunk. And as the destruction of the *Titanic* had not been anticipated, it had too few lifeboats, further increasing the number of passengers who perished in the icy waters.

BOEING

The Alaska–Yukon–Pacific Exposition in 1909 was one of the first aviation shows in America. Many spectators turned up to see for themselves that aeroplanes—as they were called back in those days—were no fiction but a reality for the future. One such spectator was William Edward Boeing, son of a German mining engineer. The young Boeing fell in love with aeroplanes at first sight, and it did not take him long to demonstrate this love: just six years later, Boeing and the engineer George Conrad Westervelt introduced their own B-1 hydro-aeroplane. At that time, their company went by the name Pacific Aero; it changed its name to Boeing one year later. In the 1920s, the Boeing Company began to produce aeroplanes for military purposes. During the Second World War, Boeing's designers introduced the Stratoliner, the first aircraft to offer a pressurized cabin, which enabled it to carry its passengers to unprecedented altitudes, thus crossing a seemingly unbreachable frontier. Some dreams simply know no bounds: the sky's the limit, as they say! No surprise, then, that the Boeing Company was later involved in the building of the International Space Station (ISS).

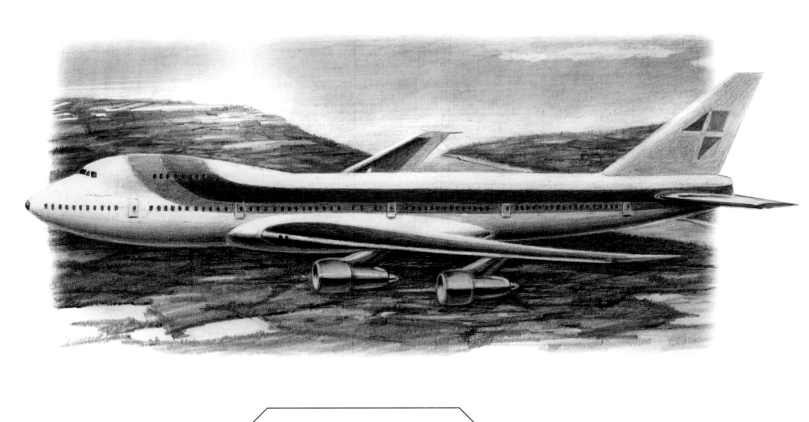

Above: Boeing 747
Below: Boeing 307 Stratoliner

BURT MUNRO'S INDIAN SCOUT

The pages of this book tell stories of people and machines that gave the world something new and unforgettable. Many of them pushed beyond the frontiers of what was thought possible. The story of New Zealander Burt Munro is an excellent case in point. His passions were speed and his Indian-brand motorbike. Having bought this bike when he was fifteen, he remained loyal to it his whole life. The Indian company was the very first in America to make motorcycles, and

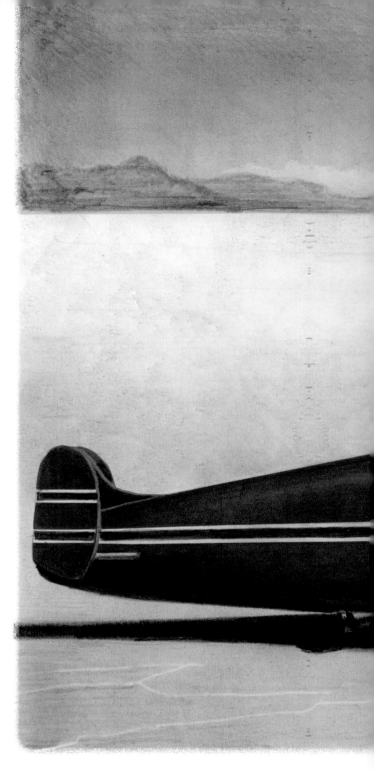

Burt Munro's story was filmed as *The World's Fastest Indian*, starring ANTHONY HOPKINS.

The modifications Burt made to his bike inspired a new Indian motorcycle, on which Burt's nephew Lee broke the land speed record.

it was the leading manufacturer of sports motorcycles for many years. The Indian Scout owned by Munro was made in 1920, the 627th bike that Indian Motorcycle produced. It is worth pointing out that its maximum speed of 55 miles per hour wasn't particularly impressive, even back then. But Munro modified and improved his beloved bike to such a degree that he and it would go on to break the land speed record with ease three times—at the Bonneville Salt Flats in Utah, where the endlessly flat landscape is a great incentive to get the most out of your machine. In an unofficial round of the competition, Munro's Scout once reached a speed of 205 mph, even higher than his hitherto unbroken record. So you could say that Burt lived out his childhood dream not just three times, but four!

TATRA 87

Tatra is the world's third oldest car-producing company with an unbroken history. In its time it has made vehicles for practically every means of transport you can think of, from trams to aircraft to snowmobiles. Before World War II, Tatra's designers, the Ledwinka brothers and Erich Überlacker, designed two automobiles that have gone down in history, each in a different way. The Tatra 87 was an aerodynamic luxury vehicle; it was the successor to the Tatra 77, the world's first aerodynamic car and an inspiration for the world-famous Chrysler Airflow. Fast as the wind (90–100 miles per hour), it was spacious enough for five people. With its comfortable armrests, high-quality upholstery, and velour floor mats, you wouldn't have minded taking it to the ends of the Earth. Which, in fact, is just what two celebrated Czech travelers did. In 1947, Miroslav Zikmund and Jiří Hanzelka loaded up a Tatra and then spent the next three years taking it all over the planet, in the process exploring remote areas of Africa and South America. As a result, the T87 made a deep impression on all their compatriots. Its younger sister, the T97, inspired the legendary Volkswagen Beetle—although the great similarity between the two caused a rift between the competing carmakers, resulting in court proceedings, as tends to happen in such cases. Because of the outbreak of World War II, however, the legal process was interrupted. In 1939, the T97 was withdrawn from sale, allowing the Beetle to take full advantage. The dispute resumed after the war, resulting in a sound defeat for Volkswagen.

Above we see a Tatra 87, with its three front headlights. Below, for comparison, we see a Tatra 97 and a Volkswagen Beetle. Although the Tatra has aerodynamic wings, the bodies of the cars are remarkably similar.

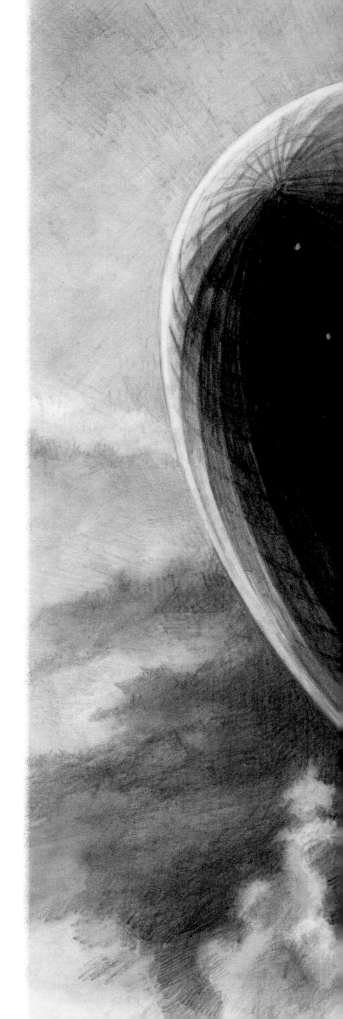

HINDENBURG

A great silver giant—about 800 feet long and 135 feet wide—floats with dignity above the clouds. The carefree, pampered passengers inside are the richest of the rich, traveling from Europe to America. And why bump your way across the sea when you can be flown to your destination in luxury and cut your travel time in half? This journey will take two and a half days; on an ocean liner it would take an arduous five. The time flies by. The passenger cabins are comfortable, and anyone who fancies a little entertainment and some company can go out to the promenade and enjoy the view, eat their fill in the dining room, even smoke a cigarette—back then nobody knew they caused lung cancer—in a smoking room carefully insulated from the rest of this celestial ship, which is kept above the clouds by more than seven million cubic feet of highly combustible hydrogen. At the slightest spark, the proud German airship the *Hindenburg* would be engulfed in flames. And, on May 6, 1937, that spark came to pass—most likely from a small discharge of static electricity. Thirty-four seconds later, the famous airship had burned to cinders. Of those on board, 36 died and 62 miraculously survived. The horrifying destruction of the *Hindenburg*—a silver *Titanic* of the skies—spelled the end of the popular yet brief era of airship travel.

BELL 47

Your parents or grandparents might remember the famous 1970s TV show *M.A.S.H.* If they do, they will also remember its theme song and the helicopter that flew wounded soldiers to the 4077th Mobile Army Surgical Hospital. Shaped like a dragonfly, this aircraft entered the history books as the first helicopter for civilian use. Its charm lay in the simplicity of its construction—a distinctive bubble-shaped cabin welded to a tail beam. In the first model, the cabin as well as the beam was uncovered, but with the passing years, various modifications and changes were made to the Bell. Although it only had a simple six-cylinder piston engine, it proved its great usefulness in many different fields—from the Apollo space program, in which it served as a trainer for a moon landing, to agriculture, in which it was involved in developing aerial crop dusting. How delighted designer Arthur M. Young must have been to see his creation employed in so many places! And just imagine the proud reaction that Renaissance artist and inventor Leonardo da Vinci, who designed a prototype helicopter in the 15th century, would have had, if he'd been alive!

Prototype aircraft for Moon-landing training, with Bell 47 cabin →

The military version of the helicopter had space in the side cabins for stretchers to carry wounded soldiers.

A typical bubble-shaped cabin with cockpit for two passengers

VOLKSWAGEN TRANSPORTER

Next time you are on your way to school, count the number of vans you see. You may be surprised by how many there are on the streets. There can be no doubt that utility vehicles play an important role in our everyday lives. Mail delivery drivers, removal companies, repairmen, police, and rescue workers—basically anyone needing to transport more than just themselves—simply can't do without a van. If we could choose only one from the inexhaustible number of vans available, we would probably choose the VW Transporter. Its first model was based on the Type 82 Kübelwagen military vehicle, which itself was based on another legend of the German automotive industry, the Volkswagen Beetle. The Type 82 was rear-wheel drive, with its engine at the back. Dutch

businessman Ben Pom came up with the idea of moving the cabin forward and making it rounder. After a few minor changes and adjustments, the Transporter would forever be associated with the 1960s and the hippie movement. Flower children in flowing clothes were so taken with the cute-looking van that they traveled from state to state in them, intent on spreading peace and love throughout the world. The end of the hippie movement didn't mean the end of the VW Transporter, though. By now it is on its sixth model, and it remains very popular into the 21st century. From time to time, we still see the very first model that harks back to the Woodstock music festival and flower power, although these days it is an oldster. It is like a familiar work of art, a much-loved museum piece.

TRIESTE

"Just imagine, we actually saw fish down there!" claimed Swiss oceanographer Jacques Piccard and US sailor Don Walsh, the first men to travel to the very bottom of the Mariana Trench in the Pacific Ocean, in the Challenger Deep on January 23, 1960. It took them four long hours to reach an impressive depth of nearly seven miles. Piccard and Walsh were mistaken in thinking they saw fish, of course. What they saw were sea cucumbers: fish cannot survive at depths greater than 5 miles. Perhaps the judgment of the two men was affected by euphoria—theirs was a remarkable first-time achievement. The intrepid explorers reached the bottom of the world's deepest sea trench in *Trieste*, a special submarine capable of traveling to great depths, known as a bathyscaphe. It was designed by the Swiss inventor Auguste Piccard, who happened to be Jacques's father. The explorers spent a full 20 minutes on the bed of the Mariana Trench. It then took them 3 hours and 15 minutes to return to the surface. A bathyscaphe

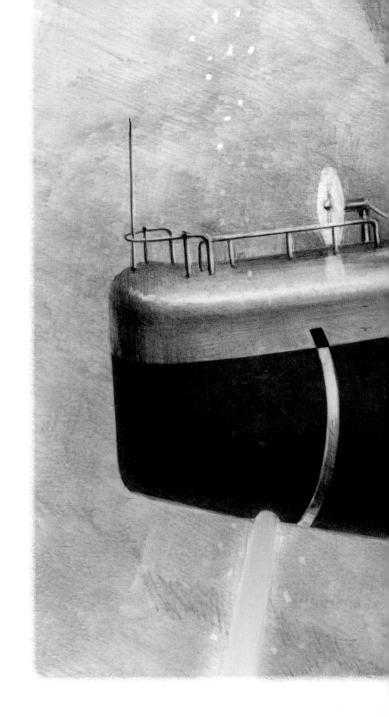

is a vessel designed to reach very great depths. The first bathyscaphe was designed and built by Auguste Piccard in 1953. Our two intrepid explorers would not have reached the bottom of the Mariana Trench in that first vessel, however, for its maximum depth was only 3.7 miles. Auguste Piccard continued to make improvements to his bathyscaphe. The shape of *Trieste* was based on that of an earlier vessel, the FNRS-2. Entered from the deck via a vertical shaft, the round nacelle attached to the bottom of the bathyscaphe served as an observation cabin for the two crewmembers, who watched what was going on around them through

thick Perspex bulbs of quartz glass illuminating the deep, dark ocean. At that time, Perspex and quartz glass were the only such materials strong enough to withstand the pressure. The bathyscaphe's fuel tank contained an unbelievable 22,000 gallons of gasoline. When the vessel reached the undersea layer known as the thermocline, it came to a halt. The remainder of its descent was managed by the buoyant force of the increasingly pressurized water. This descent could only be achieved once the crew opened a valve in the gas tank to replace some of the gas with water. But for the Perspex developing a crack, the descent went off without a hitch. The happy pioneers of the deep communicated with the crew of the auxiliary boat by transmitting sonar signals and using a hydrophone to receive sound waves underwater. Oxygen was provided by pressure cylinders, while carbon dioxide was removed by being passed through canisters of soda lime. The oceanographer Jacques Piccard was so keen on deep-sea exploration that those 20 minutes were not enough for him. He went on to make a career of it. As for *Trieste*, the first vessel to travel to such great depths, this one expedition would prove to be the only such excursion it would ever undertake.

SHINKANZEN

It is the 1950s, and Japan is faced with many challenges. One of these is the need to bring its ageing railway system up to date. The mountainous islands of this nation are interwoven with narrow rail tracks that make rapid progress impossible. Inventive engineers have long pondered how to replace slow services with modern, high-speed trains. But many people in the country see the future of transport in air travel, cars, and highways, not high-speed trains. Still the engineers, romantics all, insist on the future of the train, and they make their dreams a reality. On the occasion of the 1964 Summer Olympics in Tokyo, they introduce their very first high-speed train, on the Tokyo–Osaka line. Before long, bullet trains will be shooting across Japan at record speeds. And, of course, they will go on to inspire other countries in Asia and Europe alike. Shinkansens may be lightning fast, but they are very safe. Thanks to an ingenious system of bridges and tunnels, they avoid most obstacles that could put them in danger. Proof of this is the fact that they have never been involved in an accident that

The only moving part of the Maglev is the train itself, which maintains stability and speed along the track thanks to magnets. Hence, it needs no wheels to move at higher speeds.

The Tokyo–Osaka railway line is the world's busiest.

has claimed a human life. In addition, the Shinkansen produces a fraction of the harmful substances made by a passenger car. As speed is a part of the future, a new generation of Japanese engineers is working on a still faster train called the Maglev, which is driven by magnets that practically levitate over the track, giving the train its name. In tests, the fastest of the Maglevs has reached an incredible 374 miles per hour, almost twice the speed of an ordinary high-speed train. Celebrations would be premature, however: so far, the Maglev can manage only shorter distances, so the good old Shinkansen will keep its place in the sun for some time yet.

CAPTAIN AMERICA

What a ride! The happiest man in the world sits astride a purring chopper, racing through the American countryside. The wind lashes his face. The sun beats down. The mountains oblige him by keeping clear of the road. The scorching asphalt, peppered here and there with forgotten sand, urges him on. Absolute freedom. The gleaming motorcycle with red, white, and blue stars and stripes on the bodywork purely embodies what it means to be free. No one watching over you, no one getting in your way—all you do is ride. You're the king of the road, one of life's knights. These are the thoughts of a man eating a hamburger at a roadhouse, as he admires this parked steed. How silver it gleams! How it glows in the sun! It is Captain America, the world's most famous motorcycle, a chopper of perfect design, which became a household name as the hero of the movie *Easy Rider*—a movie about dusty roads, real hippies, and even more real freedom. Notably, Captain America mirrors the design of the police motorcycles of the day. It is mainly about the aesthetics of the thing. Gleaming handlebars, known to bikers as swallows. The super-wide front wheel span. Isn't such a bike more a work of art than a machine? Captain America is not for racing; Captain America is for enjoying everything—life, the world, the ride. Even though it is all about well-being, Jack Nicholson, one of the main actors in the movie, the one whose character doesn't do the driving, remembers that being seated on Captain America isn't as comfortable as it looks. He and his co-rider Peter Fonda were often required to cling on so tightly, for fear that the chopper would throw them from their narrow perch, that Jack once injured his ribs. Ouch! That's the price of absolute freedom. Before work on the celebrated movie began, the filmmakers had two

Wyatt's jacket

Captain Americas made from retired police bikes. One was destroyed during shooting; the other was stolen before the movie was completed. The movie was released in theaters in 1969. So who was behind the cult design of the famous bike that embodies humanity's age-old desire to be free? For a long time, Peter Fonda, the actor who

The bike was built from the Harley-Davidson HYDRA-GLIDE

took the lead role of the hippie Wyatt, believed himself responsible for it. Even though this wasn't the case, he would have been crazy to deny responsibility. In truth, Captain America is the work of Clifford "Sonny" Vaughs and the custom motorcycle builder Ben Hardy. They're the ones who assembled the bike, in consultation with Dennis Hopper and Peter Fonda. So there is the truth, and in truth there is freedom, right?

APOLLO 11 & SATURN V

In the Space Race, the Soviet Union leads the United States 1 to 0. Soviet cosmonaut Yuri Gagarin has become the first human to travel into space and return safely to Earth. As it launches its counterattack, the US predicts that by the end of the decade, a man will have walked on the moon—and that that man will be an American. In 1969, this self-confident dream will become a reality. But the preparations that have made this possible will have been anything but easy. The crew were to be catapulted into space by Saturn V, the tallest, heaviest, and most powerful rocket of all time. Saturn V had already transported six craft into space with a full record of success, and six more such successful flights would follow. "There is nothing strange or trailblazing about that," I hear you say, from your 21st-century vantage point. Well then, consider this: the computer of the super-successful Saturn V was about as powerful as today's pocket calculators, which explains why the whole mission so nearly failed. In the end, however, history was made—on June 20, 1969, for the first time a man looked at Planet Earth from the surface of the moon. "That's one small step for man, one giant leap for mankind," declared American astronaut Neil Armstrong as he raised the flag of his homeland on the moon. So what happened to the Saturn V space rocket? The only part of it to reach the moon's surface was the Lunar Module Eagle. Even that didn't make it back to the blue planet—unlike Neil Armstrong, Buzz Aldrin, and Michael Collins. The three space explorers landed back on Earth safe and sound in a tiny (10 feet wide, 6.5 feet high) remnant of a rocket that had started out 360 feet long.

The lunar module EAGLE landing on the Moon

The launch vehicle SATURN V was
composed of three main parts,
plus the Apollo spacecraft. Each
of these parts was made up of
several smaller ones. A rocket
is a bit like a jigsaw puzzle.

Neil Armstrong, Buzz Aldrin, and
ten other astronauts have walked
on the moon. All twelve were
safely returned to Earth.

CONCORDE

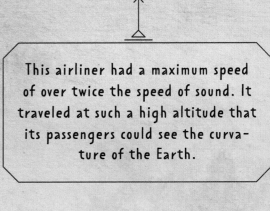

From London to New York in 3.5 hours. Around the world in 31 hours. Luxury airplanes that carry over 100 passengers at supersonic speeds. Sounds like the music of the future, doesn't it? But believe it or not, we are back in the 1980s, by which time passengers had been enjoying this splendor for several years—for thirty times the price of an ordinary flight, we should add. The price of the flight was indeed high, but the price of operating such planes was many times higher. Before such costly aircraft could soar through the skies, competitor airlines—British Airways and Air France—had to join forces. That we no longer fly at supersonic speeds has nothing to do with the price, however. In 2000, a tire on one of the aircraft burst on takeoff. Before anyone realized what had happened, the plane caught fire. The pilot failed to make an emergency landing; instead, the plane plowed into a hotel in the French town of Gonesse. Does this town sound familiar? That's right, the Concorde was not the only vehicle to meet its end in this town. (Remember the hot-air balloon in an earlier chapter in this book?) Nor is this an end to the coincidences. In the early 1970s, a Russian Tupolev Tu-144, the very first supersonic plane, was reduced to wreckage in the village of Goussainville, just a few miles from Gonesse.

This airliner had a maximum speed of over twice the speed of sound. It traveled at such a high altitude that its passengers could see the curvature of the Earth.

Supersonic aircraft stretched in size up to 10 inches in flight, owing to the heat they generated.

Russian supersonic aircraft
Tupolev Tu-144

SPACE SHUTTLE COLUMBIA

In 1969, American astronauts became the first people to walk on the Moon, thus bringing the space race to a climax. Some say the race ended in 1972, when Soviet cosmonauts and US astronauts came together in orbit as part of the Apollo–Soyuz space mission, following a cooperation agreement by the governments of the two countries. So that the bold travelers could get into orbit in the first place, a means of transport was needed not only to get them out there but also—unlike the first space rockets—to make a successful landing. In this regard, the United States remains the world leader: it has built five such space shuttles, also known as orbiters. The Soviet space shuttle *Buran*, too, made it into space, but with no crew on board. Space shuttles serve to convey materials and/or crews into orbit. They are launched into space on a rocket and slide back down to Earth when the mission ends. The first of the five US space shuttles to make it into space was *Columbia*, named after the ship *Columbia Rediviva*, the first American vessel to circumnavigate the globe, and also after the command module that landed on the moon. She was the first ship with an international crew and also the first with a female commander. Sadly, *Columbia* is often remembered for the tragic accident in 2003 that ended her career—a devastating explosion on re-entry into the Earth's atmosphere. After the accident, which resulted from a simple hole in a wing, space shuttle flights were suspended for two years. They resumed in 2005 with the space shuttle *Discovery*, which traveled successfully and accident-free until 2011, when America's Space Shuttle program was retired altogether. This doesn't mean, however, that space exploration has come to an end. In the future, rather than working in nation-state teams, countries will cooperate as we strive to reach places no one has reached before.

MEANS OF TRANSPORT THAT CHANGED THE WORLD

© Designed by B4U Publishing for Albatros,
an imprint of Albatros Media Group, 2022.
5. května 22, Prague 4, Czech Republic.
Written by Štěpánka Sekaninová & Tom Velčovský
Illustrated by Martin Sodomka
Printed in Czech Republic by FINIDR, s.r.o.
www.albatrosbooks.com

ISBN: 978-80-00-06355-3

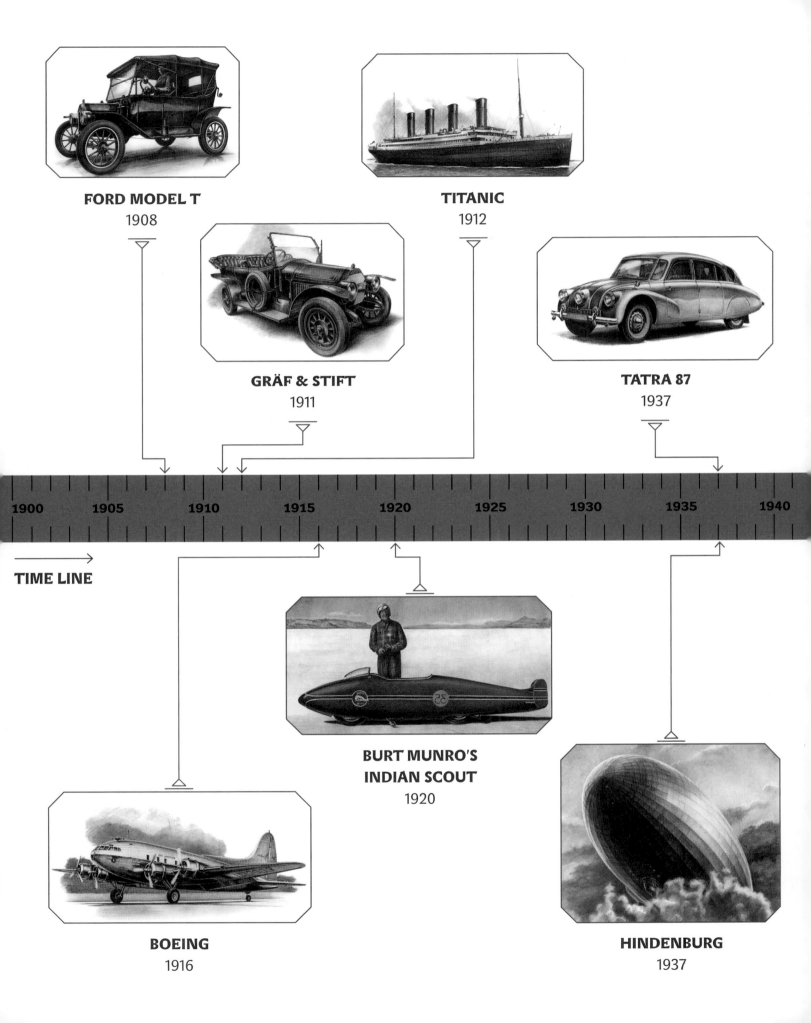

FORD MODEL T
1908

TITANIC
1912

GRÄF & STIFT
1911

TATRA 87
1937

1900 1905 1910 1915 1920 1925 1930 1935 1940

TIME LINE

**BURT MUNRO'S
INDIAN SCOUT**
1920

BOEING
1916

HINDENBURG
1937